Designed by Behram Kapadia

HAMISH HAMILTON CHILDREN'S BOOKS

Published by the Penguin Group
27 Wrights Lane, London W8 5TZ, England
Viking Penguin Inc., 40 West 23rd Street, New York, New York 10010, U.S.A.
Penguin Books Australia Ltd, Ringwood, Victoria, Australia
Penguin Books Canada Ltd, 2801 John Street, Markham, Ontario, Canada L3R 1B4
Penguin Books (N.Z.) Ltd, 182–190 Wairau Road, Auckland 10, New Zealand

Penguin Books Ltd, Registered Offices: Harmondsworth, Middlesex, England

First published in Great Britain 1983 by
Hamish Hamilton Children's Books

Copyright © 1983 by Joy Richardson (text)
Copyright © 1983 by Colin and Moira Maclean (illustrations)

All rights reserved. Without limiting the rights under copyright reserved above, no
part of this publication may be reproduced, stored in or introduced into a retrieval
system or transmitted, in any form or by any means (electronic, mechanical,
photocopying, recording or otherwise), without the prior written permission of both
the copyright owner and the above publisher of this book.

Reprinted 1985, 1986, 1987

British Library Cataloguing in Publication Data
Richardson, Joy
What happens when you grow?
1. Human growth. – Juvenile literature
I. Title
612'.6 QP84
ISBN 0 241 10970 1

Printed in Great Britain by
Cambus Litho, East Kilbride

What happens when you GROW?

Joy Richardson

Illustrated by
Colin and Moira Maclean

Hamish Hamilton · London

When you first began
you were smaller than
a grain of sand.

You were just a little egg
inside your mother.

Some tiny seeds called sperms came from your father's body. One joined up with the egg and you began to grow.

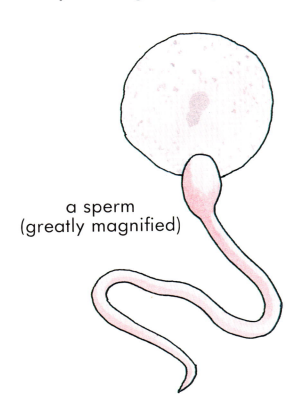

a sperm
(greatly magnified)

Your whole body is made
of tiny parts called cells.
The egg cell grew bigger
and split into two.
The two cells grew bigger
and split into four,
and so it went on.

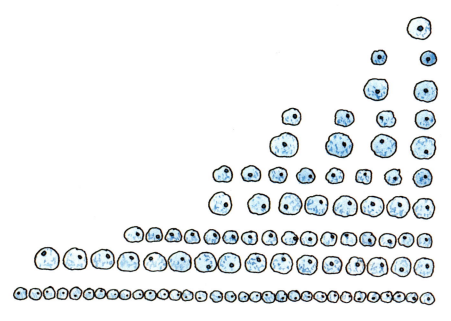

Make a ball the size of a marble
from a large lump of plasticene.
Split it into two.
Make each ball the size of a marble again.
Split them each into two.
Keep doing this for ten minutes.
How many balls have you made?
Make them into the shape of a person.

Your body grows bigger like this.

You grew inside your mother
in the part called her womb.
After two months you were
as big as a bean.
You had a head and a body
and little arms and legs.

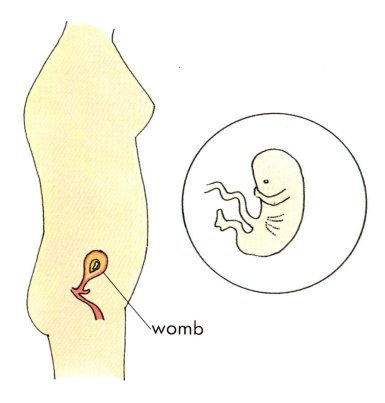
womb

After nine months you were
about 50 centimetres long.
You weighed about 3 or 4 kilograms.
You were ready to be born.

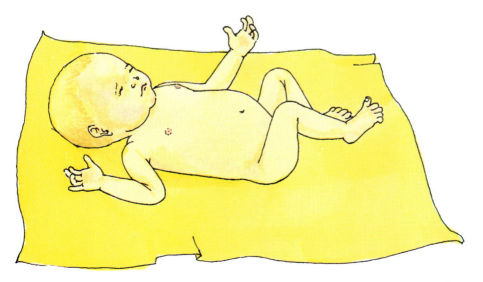

If you went on growing
as fast as you did
before you were born,
you would be as tall as a house
by the time you were ten!

Measure how tall you are now.
How much have you grown
since you were born?
How much more must you grow
to be as tall
as your mother or father?

When you were a baby
you had short soft bones.
You could not walk.
Slowly your bones grow
longer and harder.
They make you taller and stronger.

Near the ends of your bones
there are soft parts
where new bone grows.

When you are about sixteen
the soft parts harden.
Your bones stop growing.
You stop growing taller.

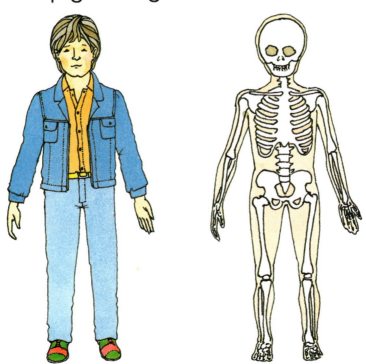

As you grow bigger
you need more skin.
Some creatures,
like snakes,
shed their skin
when it gets too small.
You change your skin
a bit at a time.
You don't notice this happening.

Your skin is made up of layers.
The top layer of skin is dead.
It flakes off bit by bit.
New skin pushes up from
underneath and takes its place.

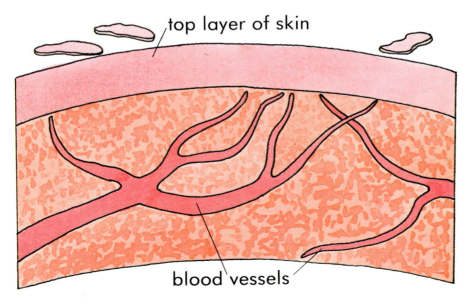

Put a piece of dark paper
on the table.
Lean over it and rub your
head hard.
Did any bits of old skin fall off?
Look at them through a
magnifying glass.

Your hair grows from roots
inside little holes in your skin.
Your hair may grow curly
or wavy
or straight.

New hair grows from the root
and pushes up out of the hole.

A hair can grow
about 20 centimetres
in a year.

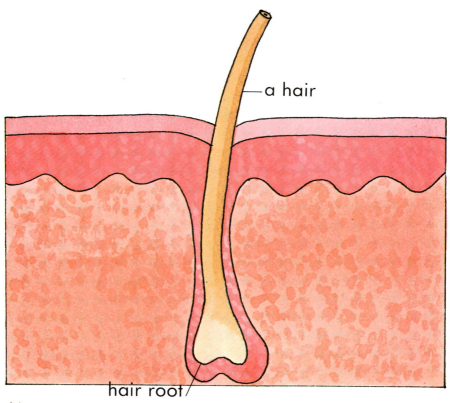

Brush your hair hard
with a clean hair brush.
Look at the brush.
How many hairs have fallen out?
Now look at them through
a magnifying glass.
Can you see the root ends?

Every day, lots of old hairs
fall out.
After a while new hairs start
growing in their place.

Your nails are made
of very tough skin.
The new part grows
under the skin
at the bottom of the nail.
It pushes up to the top.

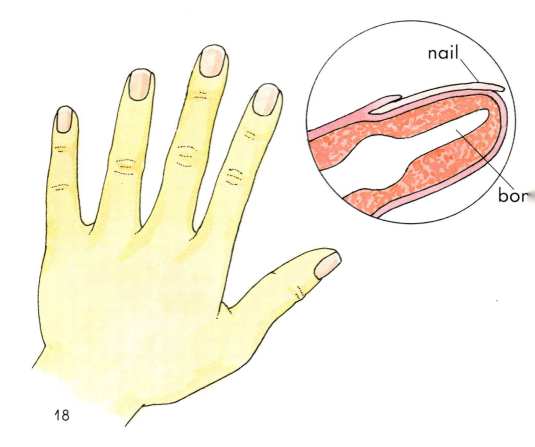

New teeth grow
inside your gums.
Your big teeth grow and make
your first teeth fall out.

How many teeth have you now?
When you are grown up, you may
have as many as thirty-two.

As you grow bigger
your body changes
in other ways too.
Girls grow breasts.
Boys grow hair on their
faces and chests.

People grow to be different sizes.
There are tall people
and short people,
fat people
and thin people.
Children often look like
other people in their family.

As you grow old
your body goes on changing.
Your skin becomes more wrinkly.
Your muscles get weaker.
Your hair goes grey.

Make a collection of photographs
of your mother or father
or grandmother or grandfather.
Put the photographs in order
from youngest to oldest.

What changes can you see?

Now think of your family.
Are you older or younger
than most of your family?

INDEX

bones   10, 11
cells   4
egg   2
hair   15, 16, 17, 22
nails   18
skin   11, 13, 14, 18, 22
sperms   3
teeth   19
womb   6